PETS AND WILD **ANIMALS**

GECKO OR KOMODO DRAGON

BY BRENNA MALONEY

Children's Press®
An imprint of Scholastic Inc.

A special thank-you to the team at the Cincinnati Zoo & Botanical Garden for their expert consultation.

GECKO

Library of Congress Cataloging-in-Publication Data available

ISBN 978-1-338-89986-3 (library binding) | ISBN 978-1-338-89987-0 (paperback)

10 9 8 7 6 5 4 3 2   24 25 26 27 28

Printed in China   62
First edition, 2024

Book design by Kay Petronio

Photos ©: cover right and throughout: Aprison Aprison/EyeEm/Alamy Images; 5 right: ANDREYGUDKOV/Getty Images; 12–13: USO/Getty Images; 15: Richard Susanto/Getty Images; 16–17: kuritafsheen/Getty Images; 18–19: BAY ISMOYO/AFP/Getty Images; 21: Jurgen & Christine Sohns/Getty Images; 22 main: Cathy Keifer/Dreamstime; 23: USO/Getty Images; 24–25: Vitaliy Halenov/Getty Images; 26–27: Michael Pitts/NPL/Minden Pictures; 28 main: Crezalyn Nerona Uratsuji/Getty Images; 30 bottom left: Vitaliy Halenov/Getty Images.
All other photos © Shutterstock.

KOMODO DRAGON

CONTENTS

MEET THE ANIMALS

Geckos and Komodo dragons are *very* different animals. Geckos are wild animals, but can be pets and live with people. Komodo dragons are wild animals that live in nature.

ADULT HUMAN

KOMODO DRAGON

GECKO

Geckos and Komodos have a few things in common. Both are **cold-blooded** animals. Their bodies are also covered with protective **scales**. Both are **reptiles**, too. Get ready to discover more about what geckos and Komodo dragons share and how they are different.

LEOPARD GECKO

KOMODO DRAGON

FACT

A Komodo dragon can live for about 50 years in the wild.

GECKO CLOSE-UP

Geckos are a type of lizard. Leopard geckos are one of the most popular lizard pets. These geckos get their name from the leopard-like spots that cover their backs. They can grow to be about 8 inches (20 cm) long and weigh about as much as a tennis ball.

LEOPARD GECKO

SKIN
Their skin is bumpy, w
tougher skin around t
heads, necks, and bac

TRICKY TAILS
A gecko's tail is about as long as its body.

HIDDEN EARS

Leopard geckos' ears are openings on either side of their heads that are covered and protected by skin.

BLINK, BLINK

Many geckos do not have eyelids, but leopard geckos do.

TINY TEETH

A leopard gecko can replace each of its small 100 teeth every three to four months.

SHORT LEGS

This lizard keeps close to the ground on short legs, which help it to move quickly.

LONG CLAWS

Leopard geckos have sharp claws on their feet. They use these claws to climb.

KOMODO DRAGON

CLEAR VISION

A Komodo can see objects nearly 1,000 feet (300 m) away. Its eyes are especially good at picking up movement from prey.

STRONG NOSE

This reptile can smell a meal up to 2.5 miles (4 km) away.

FORKED TONGUE

A Komodo dragon also smells with its long, yellow, forked tongue. Its tongue samples the air.

TEETH

Razor-sharp teeth are designed for eating. A dragon may go through four or five sets of its 60 teeth during its lifetime.

THICK SKIN
s tough skin is covered with bony plates.

TOUGH TAIL
A Komodo's tail is as long as its body. The tail is strong enough to knock down large prey.

SHARP CLAWS
Claws are used for digging and wounding prey.

KOMODO DRAGON CLOSE-UP

Did you know Komodo dragons are not actually dragons? They are a type of monitor lizard, or family of reptiles. Komodo dragons are the largest lizards in the world. They can reach 10 feet (3 m) long and weigh up to 150 pounds (68 kg). They range in color from black to yellow-gray.

9

Leopard geckos are also called leos.

FACT

INDOOR HOUSING

Leopard geckos are found in the Middle East and parts of northern India. They live in rocky, dry grassland and desert areas. But these little lizards can also be kept as pets. An old fish tank can make a good home for a gecko. Geckos need hiding places and plenty of room to climb. They need help to stay warm. A warming light can keep them comfortable.

IN THE WILD

Komodo dragons can only be found in the wild on five islands in Indonesia. Four of these volcanic islands are in Komodo National Park. The fifth island is called Flores. They are hot, with hills, forests, and grasslands. Komodo dragons rarely travel beyond the area where they hatched.

Komodo Island is home to the largest number of Komodo dragons.

GOING SOLO

Geckos prefer to live alone. They can live in groups, bu[t]
only if there is just one male per group. Males that live
together might fight.

Komodo dragons live and hunt on their own. They only come together to share a meal.

FACT
Komodo dragons can run in short bursts as fast as 12 miles per hour (19 kph).

A sick gecko will not eat.

FACT

DINING IN

Leopard geckos are **insectivores**. That means they eat insects. They feed on crickets, roaches, mealworms, beetles, and wax worms, for example. Pet owners often sprinkle powdered **nutrients** on their geckos' food.

DINING OUT

Komodo dragons are **carnivores**. That means they eat meat. They will also eat dead animals. They mostly hunt deer, pigs, rodents, monkeys, goats, wild boars, and even large water buffalo. Young Komodo dragons will eat small lizards and insects, as well as snakes and birds.

Komodo dragons can eat almost 6 pounds (3 kg) of meat in one minute.

SENDING A MESSAGE

Leopard geckos can make a variety of sounds: chirps, squeaks, barks, and screams. Chirping and squeaking are signs that a gecko is in a good mood. Geckos click whenever they feel uncomfortable or stressed.

Komodo dragons don't have much to say. Hissing is one of the few sounds that they make. A Komodo may hiss when it's attacking prey. They have other ways of speaking. A lashing tail and open mouth can send a clear message to others to stay away.

ON THE HUNT

Wild geckos rely on their sense of smell to find food.
They stalk prey and then attack with their mouths ope

Komodo dragons are **venomous** lizards. A bite from Komodo dragon is deadly.

FACT
The Gila monster and the Mexican bearded lizard are also venomous reptiles.

A striped baby gecko will shed its skin soon after hatching.

FACT

GECKO HATCHLINGS

Geckos give birth by laying eggs. A mother gecko lays two to ten eggs in one summer. After the eggs have been laid, she buries them to hide them. Gecko eggs need about 50 days to hatch. Baby geckos have a hard tip, or egg tooth, at the end of their noses. It helps them crack their eggs from the inside. The young, or **hatchlings**, can be 3 to 4 inches (8 to 10 cm) long.

KOMODO HATCHLINGS

A mother Komodo dragon lays between 15 and 30 eggs at a time. She builds and guards a nest. The eggs hatch up to nine months later. The hatchlings are born with sharp claws, which they use to climb trees. While living in trees, the babies eat eggs, grasshoppers, beetles, and geckos.

NIGHTY NIGHT

Leopard geckos are **nocturnal**. In the wild, they stay underground and sleep during the daytime. This helps them avoid the heat and the risk of getting eaten by a **predator**.

A Komodo dragon comes out of its **burrow** in the morning to look for a sunny spot to warm up in. Once warm, the dragon searches for its first meal. Then it aps in the shade during the hottest part of the day.

FACT A Komodo dragon can survive on as few as 12 meals a year.

YOU DECIDE!

Now you know what makes geckos and Komodo dragons so different! If you had to choose, would you rather be a gecko or a Komodo dragon? If you are gentle and like being around people, you may choose to be a gecko. If you want to stalk prey and hiss at your enemies, you might want to be a Komodo dragon.

GLOSSARY

burrow (BUR-oh) – a tunnel or hole in the ground made or used as a home by an animal

carnivore (KAHR-nuh-vor) – an animal that eats other animals for food

cold-blooded (KOHLD bluhd-id) – having a body temperature that changes according to the temperature of the surroundings

hatchling (HACH-ling) – a young animal that has recently emerged from its egg

insectivore (in-SEK-tuh-vor) – an animal that eats insects

nocturnal (nahk-TUR-nuhl) – active at night

nutrient (NOO-tree-uhnt) – a substance that is needed by people, animals, and plants to stay strong and healthy

predator (PRED-uh-tur) – an animal that lives by hunting other animals for food

prey (pray) – an animal that is hunted by another animal for food

reptile (REP-tile) – a cold-blooded animal that crawls across the ground or creeps on short legs; most have backbones and lay eggs

scales (skaylz) thin, flat, overlapping pieces of hard skin that cover the body of a fish or reptile

venomous (VEN-uhm-uhs) producing venom, or poison, that can pass to a victim through a bite or sting

INDEX

Page numbers [...]
indicate imag[...]

ABOUT THE AUTHOR

Brenna Maloney is the author of many books. She li[...] and works in Washington, DC, with her husband, tw[...] sons, one dog, two cats, but no reptiles. If she had to choose, she would want to be a Komodo dragon.